Enigmatic Ancient Cyprus
Land of Gods and Goddesses

Table of Contents

1. Introduction 1
2. The Dawn of Civilization: Cyprus in the Stone Ages 2
   2.1. Arrival of the First Inhabitants 2
   2.2. The Aceramic Neolithic: The Dawn of Settled Life 3
   2.3. Ceramic Neolithic: The Potter's Revolution 3
   2.4. The Chalcolithic-era: The Enigma of Copper 4
3. An Era of Bronze: Transformation and Traces 6
   3.1. The Dawn of Metallurgy 6
   3.2. Transition to Bronze 6
   3.3. The Advent of Trade 7
   3.4. Emergence of Complex Societies 7
   3.5. Bronze Age Art and Ritual Practices 7
   3.6. Decline of the Bronze Age 8
4. Gods and Goddesses: The Pantheon of Ancient Cyprus 9
   4.1. A Melting Pot of Divinities 9
   4.2. Aphrodite: The Goddess of Love 9
   4.3. Apollo Hylates: Protector of the Woodlands 10
   4.4. Zeus: The Supreme Entity 10
   4.5. Resheph-Mikal: A Peculiar Fusion 10
   4.6. Lesser-Known Divinities 11
   4.7. Cypriot Pantheon: A Unique Blend 11
5. Architecture and Iconography: Stones Telling Stories 12
   5.1. A Tapestry in Stone: Overview of the Architecture 12
   5.2. Vibrancy of the Hellenism and Roman Eras 13
   5.3. Byzantine Legacy 13
   5.4. Deciphering the Edifices: Iconography in Ancient Cyprus . . 14
   5.5. Bronze Age: Ceramic Work and Seals 14
   5.6. Hellenistic to Roman Period: Human Figures and

Mythological Themes 15
  5.7. Byzantine Iconography: Religious Themes 15
6. Cyprus and the Sea: Trade and Cultural Links 17
  6.1. The Beginnings of Maritime Activity 17
  6.2. Emergence as a Trading Hub 17
  6.3. The Iron Age Transformation 18
  6.4. Influence of Classical Civilizations 18
  6.5. Byzantine Era and Beyond 19
7. Rituals, Festivals and Mysteries: A Peek into Ancient Cypriot Life 20
  7.1. The Cult of the Great Goddess 20
  7.2. Mysteries at Kourion 21
  7.3. Spirited Festivals 21
  7.4. The Serpentine Mysteries of Golgoi 22
  7.5. Conclusion 22
8. The Confluence of Cultures: The Greeks, Egyptians, and Persians 23
  8.1. The Greeks: Heracles' Footprints and Aphrodite's Birth 23
  8.2. The Egyptians: Ambassadors of Trade and Religion ... 23
  8.3. The Persians: Conquerors and Administrators 24
  8.4. The Cultural Melting Pot 24
9. War and Peace: Shifts of Power and their Impact 26
  9.1. The Bronze Age – The Arrival of Significant Power Structures 26
  9.2. Conflict-infused Copper Trade 26
  9.3. The Arrival of the Mycenaeans 27
  9.4. The Iron Age – Power Ripples through Assyrian, Egyptian, and Persian Control 27
  9.5. Perils under the Persian Empire 28
  9.6. Alexander the Great – A Brief Respite 28

10. Art and Artistry: Aesthetic Expressions from Ancient Cyprus ... 30
    10.1. The Role of Art and Its Evolution ... 30
    10.2. The Bronze Age Revolution ... 30
    10.3. Statues and Figurines: Three-Dimensional Storytelling ... 31
    10.4. The Iron Age: Flourishing Artistry ... 31
    10.5. Cypriot Sculpture: The Influence of Gods ... 32
    10.6. The Mosaics: Attention to Detail ... 32
11. The Echoes of Ancient Cyprus: Resonances in Contemporary Life ... 33
    11.1. Landscapes Steeped in Mythology ... 33
    11.2. Language: A Mirror to Cyprus's Past ... 34
    11.3. The Vibrancy of Festivals ... 34
    11.4. Art, Architecture, and Ancient Influences ... 35
    11.5. Culinary Heritage: A Timeless Treat ... 35

Chapter 1. Introduction

Dive into the captivating mysteries of yore with our Special Report on "Enigmatic Ancient Cyprus: Land of Gods and Goddesses." Premised on the treasures and enigmas of an ancient civilization that once flourished on this island, this enthralling report will sweep you off to the age of deities and mythologies, brimming with invigorating tales and profound wisdom. Unveil the secrets hidden within the fulcrum of the Eastern Mediterranean and unravel the invigorating confluence of cultures that has transpired over millennia. Whether you're a history enthusiast, a mythological adept, or merely someone who enjoys immersing themselves in compelling narratives, this report is a vibrant tapestry of stories waiting to be unraveled. Take this journey with us and let the allure of ancient Cyprus dust off the mundane and invigorate your thirst for knowledge. Buy the report and begin this journey of discovery today!

Chapter 2. The Dawn of Civilization: Cyprus in the Stone Ages

The first echoes of civilization in Cyprus, indeed a prehistoric echo, could be traced back to ten millennia before the Common Era, when humans first stepped foot on this island. The thick veil of time conceals much of these early wanderers' lives; however, fascinating traces of their existence have been unearthed in recent archaeological explorations. Studying these enigmatic remnants grants us a glimpse into the surreal and stark world of stone-age Cyprus.

2.1. Arrival of the First Inhabitants

The maiden chapter of human habitation in Cyprus began approximately in 10,000 BCE, corresponding to the incipient Neolithic period elsewhere. Meager scraps of evidence hint that during this phase, settlers navigated in makeshift rafts or boats from the surrounding coastal regions, primarily the nearby Levantine coast. Their journey offered the first testament to humans' yearning for exploration and conquest.

The Aetokremnos site near Limassol, famous for its pygmy hippopotamus remains and few stone tools, dating between 12,000 to 10,000 BCE, might be the oldest instance of human activity on the island. However, the human aspect is still contended by scholars due to the utter rarity of evidence. Persuasive evidence of human habitation becomes far clearer in the subsequent period, known as the Aceramic or Pre-Pottery Neolithic.

2.2. The Aceramic Neolithic: The Dawn of Settled Life

Marking a significant transition from a nomadic lifestyle to a settled one, the Aceramic Neolithic period bears testimony to the humankind's first known agricultural settlement. The settlers began to engage in farming, animal rearing, fishing, and tool-making — strategies they brought from the Levant.

Sites like Khirokitia (also known as Choirokoitia) and Kalavasos-Tenta from around 7000-5000 BCE unveiled the story of these early settlers. Circular houses, consistent with Levantine architectural styles, were nestled within a system of protective walls — a sign of the emerging sophistication and the importance of collective defense system.

Even though ceramics were yet to be incorporated, the Aceramic Neolithic settlers showcased their creativity through intricate artwork carved out of stone and bone artifacts, like the famous sculpture of a cruciform woman-like figure discovered in Khirokitia. These nascent expressions of art and spirituality hint towards a slow wake of human consciousness that began to perceive something beyond mere survival.

2.3. Ceramic Neolithic: The Potter's Revolution

The invention of pottery around 4500 BCE, marking the Ceramic Neolithic period, was a tremendous technological leap in the age-old human history. With the vessels to store and transport food and water, life for the Neolithic population became significantly easier. The onset of this era could be traced back to Shillourokambos, a well-excavated site near Parekklisia.

Rhythmic spirals, hatched patterns, and representations of the natural environment adorned these pottery artifacts. In addition to the pottery, statuettes and figurines emanating spiritual and ritualistic sentiments were fashioned out of terracotta. Idols of corpulent women were the most frequently found, interpreted as symbols of a mother-goddess to signify fertility and abundance — perhaps, an absolute glimpse of the budding spirituality of these Neolithic people.

The remnants of burials, including animal and human figurines placed near the deceased, reflect the development of complex belief systems encompassing life, death, and the afterlife. The practice of burying dogs with humans, also seen at Shillourokambos, is an intriguing puzzle hinting at the ancient domestication of canines and the tender human-animal connection.

2.4. The Chalcolithic-era: The Enigma of Copper

Around 3900 BCE, we witness the emergence of the Chalcolithic era, characterized by the introduction of copper. These precious ores were initially used only for crafting ornaments, presumably due to the lack of knowledge regarding their practical properties.

This era is renowned for its fascinating range of figurines and pottery displaying intricate craftsmanship. Perhaps the most famous are plank-shaped figurines made of picrolite, a soft, greenish stone found predominately in the Troodos Mountains. The meaning and use of these peculiar figures, often adorned with incised patterns, remain yet another enigma awaiting unravelling.

As we conclude this chapter, one cannot help but marvel at how the stone-age people of Cyprus persevered through the rigors of time, pioneered revolutionary innovations, and laid the groundwork for the civilization to come. It's within these humble beginnings that the historical and cultural wealth of Cyprus is rooted, waiting patiently to be unfurled by the curious.

While much of Cyprus's stone-age history still lies buried beneath the soil and the shadows of antiquity, it serves as a constant reminder of our ancestors' resilience and innovation. As we venture forward in the story of this land, we carry with us the echoes of a past that shaped the course of human history. Whether it's the mysteries of the pygmy hippopotamus at Aetokremnos, the protective walls of Khirokitia, the pottery revolution at Shillourokambos or the enigmatic figurines of picrolite, each puzzle piece adds a new layer to the understanding of this timeless island – Cyprus, a captivating heritage journal from the stone-age past.

Chapter 3. An Era of Bronze: Transformation and Traces

As the era prior to the Iron Age, the Bronze Age in Cyprus heralded the making of a transformative period in the annals of civilization. This age, which lasted from roughly 2500-1050 B.C.E., was shaped by irrevocable changes in the facets of technology, society, and culture. During these years, Cyprus found its place on the trans-Mediterranean trade routes and gradually became a highly desirable source of copper.

3.1. The Dawn of Metallurgy

The Chalcolithic (Copper Age) was the prelude to what we understand as the Bronze Age. This era stamped the initial approach towards metallurgy. Early settlers smelted malachite to obtain pure copper, a skill which demonstrated their extraordinary grasp of advanced technologies. The production of copper objects increased substantially, leading to the creation of ornaments, tools, and weapons. As a testament to the advanced innovation of the age, these artifacts, although rudimentary, laid the groundwork for the technological leap to bronze.

3.2. Transition to Bronze

Copper is malleable, but bronze—an alloy of copper and tin or arsenic—is tougher and more enduring. The transition from copper to bronze was not immediate but occurred progressively over time. Discovery of bronze technology transformed Cyprus into an island at the pivot of metallurgical innovation. The newfound abilities to forge, cast, and craft items out of this durable medium brought about revolutionary changes.

3.3. The Advent of Trade

Once the value of the precious resource beneath the Cypriot soil was understood, the island became an active participant in the Mediterranean trade. The abundance of copper instigated a surge in commerce with neighboring civilizations, playing an important role in establishing Cyprus as an attractive trading spot. Archaeological findings have shown pottery from Mycenaean Greece, suggesting a sophisticated network of interaction and product exchange across the Aegean Sea. Even as far as the Levant, Cypriot pottery has been unearthed, cementing the island's position on maritime trade maps.

3.4. Emergence of Complex Societies

Trade and advancements in metallurgy not only drove economic growth but also triggered significant societal changes. As Cyprus proved herself a competitive force in the regional trade arena, it steered the evolution of societal hierarchy, marking the emergence of complex societies. Archaeological evidence suggests a shift towards permanent settlements and structured town planning, contributing to the rise of powerful political entities.

3.5. Bronze Age Art and Ritual Practices

Ceramics and bronze figurines from the Bronze Age mirror the aesthetic ethos and religious sentiments of the period. The intriguingly crafted statuettes uncovered from the sites, primarily of women and bulls, suggest their importance in religious and cultural narratives. The existence of sanctuaries and artefacts, such as stone horns, portray a society deeply entrenched in religious beliefs.

3.6. Decline of the Bronze Age

Despite progress and prosperity, the Bronze Age in Cyprus was not without its trials. External invasions, environmental crises, and internecine conflicts led to a prolonged phase of decline. This was particularly evident around 1200 B.C.E., when many coastal cities and settlements were deserted. The exact cause is still shrouded in mystery, suggesting widespread instability that eventually led to the end of this invigorating era.

The Bronze Age was the transformative period that significantly shaped the future of Cyprus. Shifts in technological capabilities, the evolution of societal structures, growth in trade, and cultural development all vitally contributed to laying the foundation on which the great civilization of ancient Cyprus was built. The vestiges and lore of this bygone era continue to reveal a fascinating journey, casting insightful light on the diverse, cultured roots that remain an integral part of Cyprus' identity today.

Chapter 4. Gods and Goddesses: The Pantheon of Ancient Cyprus

In the panorama of ancient civilizations, few are as intriguing as that which developed on the island of Cyprus. A fascination with the celestial saw the ancients of this land erect a pantheon, a divine assembly of gods and goddesses whose stories permeate the annals of time.

4.1. A Melting Pot of Divinities

Ancient Cypriots inherited their spiritual beliefs and customs from generations gone by, blending them with influences from the diverse cultures that came in contact with the island. The result is a pantheon that dips its ladle into the rich broths of Egyptian, Anatolian, Mesopotamian, and Greek mythology. This multicultural collage of deities was a testament to the island's vital position on the map of the ancients, where East met West, and realms came together in a vibrant blending of philosophies and beliefs.

4.2. Aphrodite: The Goddess of Love

By all counts, the most venerated and widely recognized deity in the ancient Cypriotic pantheon was Aphrodite, the goddess of love and beauty. Ironically, Cypriots didn't inherit her from the Greeks but rather gifted her to them. In fact, her origins can be traced back to the prehistoric love goddess of the Near East, associated with fertility and reproduction. In Cyprus, she was often portrayed as Aphrodite Paphia, drawing her title from Paphos, where her most important sanctuary stood.

4.3. Apollo Hylates: Protector of the Woodlands

Enter Apollo Hylates, the Cypriot manifestation of the god Apollo, fused with elements of the eastern nature god Resheph. As the epithet 'Hylates' suggests, Apollo was worshipped in Cyprus as a protector of the woodlands, not merely relegated to the spheres of music, poetry, and prophecy as in Greek mythology. At Kourion, one can still witness the remnants of the temple dedicated to Apollo Hylates, which prospered between 1st century BC and 2nd century AD.

4.4. Zeus: The Supreme Entity

No conversation about gods in any part of the ancient Hellenic world can be complete without mentioning Zeus, the father of gods and men. Among the Cypriots, Zeus was venerated as Zeus Olympios and was considered the supreme deity. Evidence from artifacts suggests that he was worshipped both in his classic Greek form and in a hybrid form influenced by the Canaanite god Baal.

4.5. Resheph-Mikal: A Peculiar Fusion

Resheph-Mikal or Malakbel represents an intriguing cultural blend, intertwining Semitic deities Resheph and Mikal. In the Roman period, this particular divinity was identified with Sol Invictus, the unbeatable Sun. He was a horseman deity, a bringer of victory, and a protector against evil forces. A shrine dedicated to him can be found in Kition.

4.6. Lesser-Known Divinities

There were countless other deities revered by the Cypriots, the lesser-known often linked with nature, fertility, or embodying specific local contexts. For instance, Eileithyia was the goddess of childbirth, revered mainly in Paphos, while Nemesis was the divine personification of fair retribution, and her Hellenistic sanctuary still stands at Agia Varvara.

4.7. Cypriot Pantheon: A Unique Blend

The tapestry that is the Cypriot pantheon offers a fascinating glimpse into the beliefs and philosophies of our ancestors. It highlights not only their worldview but also their interactions with other cultures. Conquering nations often brought their gods with them, but instead of replacing the native ones, these new entries only expanded and enriched the pre-existing pantheon. The result is a unique collection of deities, a divine fusion of traditions and cultures that epitomizes the spirit of ancient Cyprus itself.

The expansive pantheon shaped by the ancient Cypriots invites us to delve deeper into the mysteries of the past. It underscores the symbolic value assigned to natural elements in the island's folklore and offers glimpses of forgotten truths. After all, these gods and goddesses, a synonym for the forces beyond human control, embody the awe and reverence the ancients felt for the world around them and remain a testament to the glorious civilization that bloomed on a tiny island in the heart of the Mediterranean.

Chapter 5. Architecture and Iconography: Stones Telling Stories

Emerging from the casements of time, hallowed within the heart of the Eastern Mediterranean, Cyprus holds the remnants of a civilization manifested in its monumental relics and a testament to a long-lost era teeming with intricacies of history and culture. Two defining elements that can provide a panoramic view of this civilization are its architecture and iconography. Together, they narrate tales that are as concrete as the stones that built their grand structures and as vivid as the depictions embellishing their walls.

5.1. A Tapestry in Stone: Overview of the Architecture

The architectural heritage of ancient Cyprus is a meandering mélange of colors, designs, and cultures. It is practically a tangible canvas portraying the skill, values, beliefs, and societal growth of the Cypriot populace from antiquity.

One of the earliest architectural remnants date back to the Neolithic age, from 7000 to 6000 BC, characterized by round houses constructed from sun-dried mud bricks and flat stone foundations. As society gradually began to progress, so did their skills, and by the Chalcolithic period, they were erecting more complex architectural structures, such as rectangular houses, with plastered floors and walls.

However, it was during the Bronze Age, from approximately 1650 to 1050 BC, that Cypriot architecture made a quantum leap with urban settlements, fortification systems, and sanctuary complexes. This period was characterized by the layout of streets, advanced hydraulic systems, reinforced walls with megalithic stones, and the prominent use of ashlar masonry.

Late Bronze Age was marked by extensive monumental architecture with cities like Enkomi, Hala Sultan Tekke, and Kition exhibiting grand buildings including palaces and temples adorned with frescoes and numerous artifacts, indicating economic prosperity and powerful rulers.

5.2. Vibrancy of the Hellenism and Roman Eras

Witnessing the silent passage of centuries, Cyprus entered the Hellenistic era following the conquest by Alexander the Great. Intricate structures began to spring up, exhibiting a prominent influence of Greek architecture. There was a shift towards the use of limestone and conglomerate, managing to give a striking visual enhancement to the structures.

The arrival of the Romans around the 1st century BC led to the expansion of cities with new architectural elements. Large public buildings, agoras, theaters, amphitheaters, baths, and elaborate villas- all modeled on Roman architectural styles- embellished the cities of Kourion, Salamis and Paphos among others. Iconic edifices such as the House of Dionysus in Paphos, bear intricate mosaics telling mythological tales, a testimony to the grandeur of Roman influence.

5.3. Byzantine Legacy

The next key phase of architectural development occurred during the Byzantine period. From the 4th century to the 12th century AD, the island experienced a plethora of architectural creativity. There burgeoned a multitude of basilicas with serene atriums and beautifully paved mosaics, distinct chapels, and grand domed structures, the Byzantine churches featuring splendid artistic ornamentations.

One of the finest examples of this period's architecture is the Church of Agia Paraskevi in Yeroskipou near Paphos, a five-domed cross-in-square church, rich with mural ornamentation, exemplifying Byzantine influence intermixed with local elements.

5.4. Deciphering the Edifices: Iconography in Ancient Cyprus

No investigation into ancient architecture can be complete without a detailed study of iconography. A parallel narration surfaced through engraved symbols and images on monuments, iconography serves as an essential tool in understanding the religious, mythological, and cultural milieu of the era.

5.5. Bronze Age: Ceramic Work and Seals

The iconography from the Bronze Age was prevalent mainly in ceramic work and seals. Emblematic motifs such as birds, bulls, and double-headed idols appear to have held particular significance, with bulls symbolizing strength and fertility. Interestingly, the iconography from this era rarely depicts the human form.

5.6. Hellenistic to Roman Period: Human Figures and Mythological Themes

The dawn of the Hellenistic and Roman periods brought with them a shift in the artistic focus towards human figures and narratives from mythology. Mosaics proliferated, with many of the splendid ones found in the palatial villa, House of Dionysus in Paphos. The mosaics, often residing in the floors of the houses, exhibited an amalgamation of local and Hellenistic traditions.

5.7. Byzantine Iconography: Religious Themes

The Byzantine period heralded a new wave in iconography, with religious themes taking center stage, embodying the Christian faith. Frescoes and mosaics depicting biblical narratives and figures emerged, installed in basilicas and churches. The Church of Agia Paraskevi and the iconic painted churches of the Troodos region with their intricate frescoes stand as classic episodes of Byzantine iconography.

As we advance towards understanding the destination that is Ancient Cyprus, we must appreciate the journey that is the Cypriot architecture and iconography. With each stone cut and each symbol carved, we get a peek into the depths of an enthralling history that has significantly shaped the Cypriot identity on the Mediterranean tapestry.

Undeniably, stones have stories to tell. They bear the weight of the years gone by, patiently waiting for us to decipher, decode, and appreciate the tales of visions, values, victories, and ventures nestled within their silent structures. Explore these architectural marvels and iconographic relics as silent storytellers, illuminating and guiding our understanding of Ancient Cyprus.

Chapter 6. Cyprus and the Sea: Trade and Cultural Links

Situated at the crossroads of the eastern Mediterranean, Cyprus commanded a prominent place in regional sea routes, serving as a bustling hub for both trade and cultural exchange.

The narrative of Cyprus and the sea is deeply intertwined, with seafaring being one of the principal means by which this island carved its niche in the annals of history. Cyprus was never an isolated entity; rather, it was a veritable crossroads of commerce and culture, its shoreline embraced by the waves of different civilizations and their stories.

6.1. The Beginnings of Maritime Activity

Maritime activity in Cyprus can be traced back to the prehistoric period, during the Neolithic Age (7000-3900 BC). Archaeological studies reveal limited evidence from this era; however, it's worth mentioning the ample evidence of marine resources, underscoring the connection of early Cypriots with the sea. Fish and shellfish residues in Neolithic habitations indicate the harvesting of marine resources, an activity that likely contributed to early maritime capabilities.

6.2. Emergence as a Trading Hub

Due to its strategic location, Cyprus played an instrumental role in the Bronze Age (ca. 2400-1050 BC). It was at this juncture that Cyprus became a crucial intermediary in the complex web of trade networks, most notably in the exchange of copper (named after the island itself), ivory, pottery, and other exotic goods.

Seafaring cultures such as the Mycenaeans, Hittites, and Egyptians viewed Cyprus as an essential stopover during their sea voyages. This positioning bred a natural predilection for establishing robust trade links with these cultures. Evidence from archaeological excavations, for instance, unearthed Egyptian artifacts in Enkomi and Ugarit, substantiating the existence of a vibrant trade.

6.3. The Iron Age Transformation

The Iron Age ushered in a distinct era of transformation for Cyprus (1050-750 BC) in terms of maritime trade and cultural links. The islanders, in addition to fostering ties with neighboring coastal lands, now purposefully extended their reach, establishing colonies in far-flung areas like the Levant and Crete. The unity of Cyprus under a single monarchy during the 8th century BC further propelled the island's status as a leading player in the Mediterranean marketplace.

Huge quantities of Cypriot ceramics found along the Levantine coast and the presence of local Levantine pottery in Cypriot settlements prove that an active maritime trade network existed. It was through such networks that the diffusion of alphabetic writing and iron technology also took place.

6.4. Influence of Classical Civilizations

The classical period (475-325 BC) bore witness to the profound influence of Hellenic civilization on the island. Amidst the surge in trade, came an inflow of cultural ideas, with substantial shifts observed in religious practices, art forms, and linguistic patterns. The wide distribution of Cypriot specimens of Attic pottery, along with the establishment of Greek city-kingdoms, point to this cultural transformation.

Subsequently, with the advent of the Hellenistic Period (ca. 323-30 BC), Cyprus fell under the sphere of influence of the Ptolemaic Dynasty based in Alexandria, and maritime activity continued to flourish. Extensive underwater explorations revealed 'ship-sheds' and anchorage sites, bearing evidence to the wealth and activity of the Ptolemaic naval base.

6.5. Byzantine Era and Beyond

The Byzantine era (AD 395-1191) was significant for Cyprus, with the island operating as a critical naval base during the early medieval period. Cyprus became a pivotal point in the region's commercial network, linking the eastern Mediterranean economies and allowing for increased interaction and exchange between diverse cultures and religions.

Explorations into the subsequent Venetian, Ottoman, and British periods point to an ongoing development, with Cyprus continuing to prosper in maritime trade and cultural exchanges.

In retrospect, Cyprus' history is inextricably linked to the sea, the silent observer and catalyst that has played a significant role in the shaping of this enigmatic island. The waters surrounding Cyprus witnessed the rise and fall of empires, securing the island's position as a hub of sea trade routes throughout different epoch, continuously nourishing its rich cultural diversity. The maritime traditions developed over millennia continue to pervade the island's identity, invigorating the irresistible call of the sea that echoes across the ages.

Chapter 7. Rituals, Festivals and Mysteries: A Peek into Ancient Cypriot Life

Ancient Cyprus played a significant role in the cultural and spiritual development of the proto-European Mediterranean world. Cultures ebbed and flowed across this sunny island, each leaving a unique stamp on its vibrant tapestry of life, especially in the realm of rituals, festivals, and mysteries. This chapter seeks to explore this corner of Ancient Cypriot life, shedding light on the practices that shaped the society and its faith over centuries.

7.1. The Cult of the Great Goddess

The Great Goddess, a deity of fertility, nature, and animals, was central to the religious life in ancient Cyprus. Her representation often combined elements from the Hellenistic Artemis, the Phoenician Astarte, and even the Egyptian Isis, demonstrating the multicultural nature of the island. Temples dedicated to her were typically of an open-air design, with sacred sanctuaries often positioned on hilltops or in nature, away from populated areas, aggregating divine energy and harmony with the environment.

Rituals to the Great Goddess would differ based on the season and surrounding natural events. Springtime saw grand offerings of grain, flowers, and young animals to ensure a fruitful harvest and her continued goodwill. These ceremonies usually featured joyous music, dance, and often acted as community gatherings that encouraged unity and cooperation among the local populace.

7.2. Mysteries at Kourion

Kourion, a city along the southern coast, was famous for its Sanctuary of Apollo Hylates. Here, the mysteries of Apollo were performed, an integral rite in the spiritual life of every citizen. Initiation into these mysteries occurred once one had reached adulthood, symbolising their transition into full members of the community.

Ceremonies consisted of potential initiates gathering in the evening at the sanctuary, robed in simple white tunics. As their families watched, each candidate would embark on a torchlit procession into the heart of the site, symbolically moving toward enlightenment. Dancing, singing, and an offering to Apollo were part of the ceremony, along with a secret rite known only to the participants.

7.3. Spirited Festivals

Ancient Cyprus was a land of festive joy, a salute to the bounties of nature and the favor of gods. The most significant festival was the Anthesteria, a springtime celebration dedicated to Dionysus, the god of wine and euphoria. Wine, like many products of the fertile Cypriot lands, held considerable as symbolic imports for the native population.

This grand festival saw the whole community coming together, irrespective of class or age distinctions, making it a cornerstone of ancient Cypriot culture. On the first day of the Anthesteria, people would bring offerings of newly opened wine and seasonal blooms to local temples, uttering prayers of thanksgiving. The second day was known as the day of "drinking", and fermented prune juice was freely available. The final day was reserved for more solemn rituals, including a special feast for the deceased.

7.4. The Serpentine Mysteries of Golgoi

The city of Golgoi housed another profound mystery, the enigmatic Cult of the Serpent. The serpent was a critical image in the ancient religious iconography of Cyprus. In Golgoi, excavations have uncovered coils of clay snakes entwined around altars, suggesting these reptiles' significance in religious rituals.

Exactly what the rituals entailed remains obscure due to lack of written records. Still, it's theorized that they may have involved live serpents, revered as earthly embodiments of gods or spirits, participating in ceremonial rites. Likely linked to rain and fertility rituals, serpents' shedding skin may have symbolized renewal, rebirth, and the cyclic nature of life.

7.5. Conclusion

The spiritual and festive life of ancient Cyprus brought unity to its diverse populace. These practices were an embodiment of shared respect for nature, divine entities, and societal bonds. These rituals, festivals, and mysteries are not mere historical footnotes. They continue to echo in modern Cypriot life, serving as a tangible connection to their rich and enigmatic past.

In so doing, ancient Cyprus offers us a unique window into the ways cultures are perpetually shaped and reshaped by their encounters with each other and with nature. This legacy continues to intrigue, offering profound insights into the past and the timeless lessons it imparts to the present.

Chapter 8. The Confluence of Cultures: The Greeks, Egyptians, and Persians

To truly apprehend the layered complexity of ancient Cyprus, one must delve into the confluence of cultures that has seeped into its crevices over time. This convergence is best exemplified by the arrival and influence of three prominent cultural behemoths of antiquity: the Greeks, the Egyptians, and the Persians.

8.1. The Greeks: Heracles' Footprints and Aphrodite's Birth

The Greek influence on Cypriot culture is paramount and intricately woven into both its mythology and history. Cyprus holds a special place in Greek Mythology: it is said to be where the mighty Heracles left his footprints, and, more notably, the seafoam-birthplace of Aphrodite, the goddess of love and beauty.

Historically, Cyprus came under Aegean influence around the Late Bronze Age, becoming an integral part of the Mycenaean civilization by the twelfth and eleventh centuries B.C. While Cypriot city kingdoms paid Homeric tribute to Mycenae, they assimilated the Greek language, script (Cypro-Minoan), and facets of the material culture, including pottery styles and metallurgy.

8.2. The Egyptians: Ambassadors of Trade and Religion

The Cypriots' contact with Egypt dates back to the third millennium B.C., notably marked by the sherds of Cypriot pottery found in

Egyptian archaeological sites. The relationships between these two Mediterraneans were primarily driven by trade; Cyprus was rich in copper and timber, both vital commodities for the Egyptian civilization.

Beyond the material exchanges, the Cypriot-Egyptian connections displayed a religious and cultural synthesis as well. The Cypriots incorporated Egyptian deities into their pantheon; for instance, Resheph, the Canaanite-Phoenician god of plagues was conflated with the Egyptian god Seth. Also, Cypriot art, especially statuary and steles, show Egyptian influence in design and methodology.

8.3. The Persians: Conquerors and Administrators

The Persian influence arrived in 545 B.C. after Cyprus came under the sovereignty of the Persian Empire. Despite the initial conflict, Cyprus found itself benefiting from the Persians' advanced administrative and political infrastructure. Their superior systems enabled better governance, infrastructure, and tax collection. The island's city-kingdoms maintained a level of autonomy under a federal system, while the Persians provided military protection in return for financial tribute.

Interestingly, the Persians didn't leave an overwhelmingly sensory cultural footprint on Cyprus. Instead, their influence is noted in the administrative, political realms, and certain architectural manifestations: for example, the Persian palace at Vouni with its unique architectural ensemble layout is noteworthy.

8.4. The Cultural Melting Pot

This confluence of Greek, Egyptian, and Persian influences gave Cyprus a rich, layered heritage. It morphed into the Cypriot culture, blending various elements from each of these civilizations yet distinctively unique in its identity.

This cultural mélange manifested in various forms: in the multilingual inscriptions found in ancient tombs, the hybrid architectural styles of temples and palaces, the iconography on pottery and statues, the melting pot of gods and goddesses, the fusion that could be tasted in the local cuisine, or indeed heard in the lyrical Cypriot dialect that still echoes Greek, while whispering of other influences from the past.

To unearth this confluence of cultures is to discover the soul of Cyprus, an island that made a virtue out of its geographic centrality and turned itself into a crucible of civilizations. However, it is not just its past that is defined by this confluence. These undercurrents have continued to pulse through Cyprus's veins, shaping its present and propelling it into the future. Ancient Cyprus is not a static, dry relic of history; it is a living, breathing, and evolving entity that reverberates with the echoes of the myriad cultures that have crisscrossed its terrain.

Chapter 9. War and Peace: Shifts of Power and their Impact

The history of ancient Cyprus is replete with intersecting narratives of varied civilizations; a tapestry woven with the threads of trade, conquest, conflict, domination, and resilience. This chapter delves into the shifts of power in this region, the warfare that resulted from these changes, and the consequential aftermath that shaped Cyprus as we know it.

9.1. The Bronze Age – The Arrival of Significant Power Structures

The Bronze Age marked the inception of considerable power structures in ancient Cyprus. Before this, during the Chalcolithic Era, Cypriot communities were primarily agrarian societies with little emphasis on hierarchical power. It was in the Bronze Age, roughly around 2300 BC, that Cyprus began to witness significant shifts of power brought about by the rise of city kingdoms.

These city-kingdoms, often fortified and exceedingly wealthy, began to control and monopolize the island's highly valued copper resources. This led to a power struggle amongst these city-kingdoms and subsequently ignited a rather complicated series of territorial conflicts.

9.2. Conflict-infused Copper Trade

Title reserved for city-king monarchs, like the Alasyian king, were indicative of the escalating tensions. The Bronze Age was hence named for the booming copper production and trade which became the backbone of their economy and a major player in power dynamics. Nations seeking copper were often ready to wage wars for control over this lucrative resource.

Territorial conflicts, combined with the wealth amassed from copper trade, fueled the rise of local military forces. Archaeological evidence showcases advanced defensive architectures and weaponry, signifying that the city-kingdoms were preparing for, or maybe already engaged in, frequent skirmishes or full-blown conflicts.

9.3. The Arrival of the Mycenaeans

The course of conflict and power shifts began to twist in a new direction with the arrival of the Mycenaeans around 1400 BC. Military advancements, combined with a sophisticated hierarchical structure, allowed the Mycenaeans to gradually dominate over native city-kingdoms. Their influence was so profound that the local communities began to adopt Mycenaean language, practices, and religion.

However, the conquest by Mycenaeans wasn't entirely hostile. There were periods of peace and cultural mingling. The Mycenaean flavor can be discerned in the ancient Cypriotic art, burial rites, and even in their pottery style. Yet, beneath these layers of cultural assimilation, seeds of conflict were undoubtedly brewing.

9.4. The Iron Age – Power Ripples through Assyrian, Egyptian, and Persian Control

The Iron Age turned a new leaf in the tumultuous saga of Cyprus' power shifts. Assyrian inscriptions from the 8th century BC signified a new epoch of foreign dominations that lasted almost a millennium.

Despite periods of relative peace and prosperity, Cyprus was invariably caught betwixt the tyrannies of mighty empires, leaving indelible imprints on the Cypriot culture and society.

Paradoxically, these epochs of submissive peace under foreign rule also bolstered the development of Cypriot cultural identity. Greek ascendency, for instance, engendered visible shifts in Cypriot societal practices, transforming their language, script, and religious practices significantly.

9.5. Perils under the Persian Empire

The Persian conquest of the island around 545 BC threw Cyprus into a vortex of rebellions and warfare. Although there were moments of peace, they were routinely disrupted by the spurts of rebellions against the Persian hegemony. The long stretch of Persian rule, brought severe repression, leading to infamous revolts, such as the Ionian Revolt in 499 BC and the Cypriot Rebellion in 392 BC. The relentless tug of wars for control and independence consistently challenged the status quo, adding new dimensions to the Cypriot saga.

9.6. Alexander the Great – A Brief Respite

The arrival of the Macedonian king, Alexander the Great, in 333 BC ushered in a brief period of peace for the war-riddled island. Alexander's victory over Persians not only liberated Cyprus but also brought about an era of relative stability before the island plunged into the throes of the Wars of the Diadochi, subsequent Ptolemaic rule, and the eventual annexation by the Romans.

The ancient history of Cyprus, hence, stands as a testament to the incessant persistence of the human spirit amid enduring shifts of power and relentless warfare. These alternating epochs of war and peace have not only shaped the political history of this island but also etched a rich, unique cultural identity deeply influenced by the confluence of various civilizations.

Chapter 10. Art and Artistry: Aesthetic Expressions from Ancient Cyprus

In the realm of the ancient world, the island of Cyprus served as a beacon of artistic expression and ingenuity. The geographical location of the landscape, bridging the Oriental East with the Occidental West, sanctified Cyprus as an intricate fusion of cultural influences which shaped its art and aesthetics.

10.1. The Role of Art and Its Evolution

Art in ancient Cyprus wasn't merely an act of self-expression or recreation; it performed significant roles in religious contexts, societal flows, and connotations of wealth and power. It evolved with the dawn of the Bronze Age, when skilled Cypriot artisans began creating intricate designs on pots. Their early works, imbued by simplicity and practicality, gradually developed into more sophisticated and elaborate masterpieces.

10.2. The Bronze Age Revolution

The Bronze Age (2500-1050 BC) epoch witnessed the advent of complex and sophisticated art forms. During the early phase of this era, typically referred to as Early and Middle Cypriot periods, ceramics made their conspicuous emergence with Red Polished Ware, being a notable example. Characterized by its distinctive lustrous finish, it reflects the skillful manipulation of clay and showcases intricate design patterns.

Later, with the advent of the Late Cypriot period, an influx of curvilinear and concentric circles began adorning pottery – eventually leading to the unrivaled achievement known as Base Ring Ware. Accented by a luscious chocolate-brown slip, these aesthetically pleasing works often portrayed hunting scenes or regal motifs. The evolution of the Bichrome Ware, displaying assiduous craftsmanship with its polychrome painted patterns over white slip, adds an additional layer to the grandeur.

10.3. Statues and Figurines: Three-Dimensional Storytelling

Parallel to the growth of ceramics, the Bronze Age marked the manifestation of figural statues, serving as an essential conduit for religious expression. Sanctuaries replete with terracotta statuettes bear testimony to their spiritual significance. These figurines, both anthropomorphic and zoomorphic, illustrate an intimate relationship between the Cypriots and their gods. The most distinctive are the plank-shaped figures, ranging from simple representations to those detailing facial characteristics and dress.

10.4. The Iron Age: Flourishing Artistry

From 1050-30 BC, during the Iron Age, artistry continued to flourish as craftsmen experimented with diversified mediums of sculpting. Limestone, marble, and terracotta were infused into creations, producing stunning statues and relief-decorated sarcophagi.

Pottery styles further developed and diversified, with White Painted Ware and Black Slip Ware vying for predominance. The White Painted Ware, with its stylized birds and animals over a polished white background, served as an artistic rendition of Cypriot fauna.

Meanwhile, the Black Slip Ware, characterized by geometric and linear designs, provided an elegant and more austere alternative.

Substantial influence from the Greeks is evident during this era. The Black-on-Red ware, replete with complex spiral motifs on red slip, and the Free Field Style, with animals and figures painted against a white background on vessels, exemplify the seamless Greek integration into Cypriot art.

10.5. Cypriot Sculpture: The Influence of Gods

Cypriot sculpture reflected the islanders' religious fervor, mirroring effigies of celebrated gods and goddesses. The ethereal statue of Aphrodite, touted as the Cypriot Sculpture Par Excellence, stands testament to the deity's spiritual supremacy and the islanders' deep-seated veneration.

10.6. The Mosaics: Attention to Detail

The enduring legacy of Cypriot artistry is perhaps best represented in the island's mosaic floors. Their detailed geometric motifs, intricately worked floral designs, and vivid depictions of mythology narrate silent tales of immaculate craftsmanship. The House of Aion and the House of Dionysos in Paphos are spectacular exhibitions of this art form, featuring mosaics that add dimension to the mythological tales.

Ancient Cyprus, with its panoply of artistic expressions, beckons us to appreciate and understand the depth of its history, culture, and mythology. Striding from the Bronze Age to the Hellenistic period, the island's aesthetic contributions illuminate a civilization enmeshed in artistic brilliance and cultural richness.

Chapter 11. The Echoes of Ancient Cyprus: Resonances in Contemporary Life

As an island nestled at the cross-section of cultures, Cyprus boasts a monumental legacy, significantly impacted by the whispers of ancient tales and myths. These echoes reverberate in the facets of contemporary Cypriot life, be it traditions, customs, arts, language, and much more. The cradle of civilization, it holds a captivating mix of the old world's charm and the new's vibrancy, representing a unique confluence of history and modern life. Steeped in a rich tapestry of culture, the island of Cyprus serves as a beacon to understand the modern world's underpinnings through an ancient lens.

11.1. Landscapes Steeped in Mythology

Nestled in the heart of the Mediterranean, Cyprus's landscapes are dotted with remnants of its rich historical and mythological past. Take Aphrodite's Rock (Petra tou Romiou), a picturesque sea stack on the island's western coast, considered the mythical birthplace of the Greek goddess of love, Aphrodite, in ancient legend. This captivating site, despite its tourist appeal, holds a deep resonance within the Cypriot psyche. The belief in the rock's magical qualities to endow grace, beauty, and allurement to those who swim around it thrice is popular, reflecting the enduring influence of ancient mythologies.

Similarly, Mount Olympus, the highest peak in Cyprus, resonates with ancient mythology. Although it isn't the legendary dwelling of the Greek gods, it's nonetheless imbued with a unique aura of divine reverence and fostered as a symbol of other-worldly grandeur much like its namesake on the Greek mainland.

11.2. Language: A Mirror to Cyprus's Past

The Cypriot language serves as an indelible testament to its regal past. Distinct Cypriot-Greek dialects hint at archaic Greek influences, weaving a linguistic tapestry that extends back thousands of years. It's not uncommon to hear words reminiscent of Homeric Greek in everyday conversation, carrying forward the echoes of a past golden age. The linguistic nuances, like the occasional sprinkling of Turkish and Arabic words, are veritable markers of the intermingled cultures that have etched their influences on the island over millennia.

11.3. The Vibrancy of Festivals

In Cyprus, the spectrum of festivals celebrated is a kaleidoscope of cultural resonances that find their roots in ancient rituals. The Anthestiria Flower Festival, reputedly connected to the ancient festival of Anthesteria, celebrated in ancient Athens in honour of Dionysius, God of wine and fertility, is a prime example. Modern Cypriots celebrate this festival with the same gusto as the ancients, including float parades filled with flowers, rejoicing the rebirth of nature.

Another such remarkable festival is Kataklysmos, or the Festival of the Flood. It's a unique blend of Christian traditions and ancient celebrations dedicated to Aphrodite and Adonis. The traditions associated with this festival, including water-based games and rituals, resonate with the ancients' spirit, emphasizing the seamless integration of the old and new.

11.4. Art, Architecture, and Ancient Influences

The architectural landscape of Cyprus is an enduring testament to its rich former days. From village houses that carry a strong Venetian influence to Byzantine monasteries and Gothic castles standing testimony to the island's captivating history, each structure encapsulates an aspect of the past, contributing to the cultural chronicle of this island nation.

Cypriot handicrafts, such as the intricate Lefkara lace and aphrodite's charm jewellery, reflect a heritage seeped in ancient traditions. Many modern artists and craftsmen continue to draw inspiration from themes, symbols, and mythology prevalent in the ancient world, showcasing those echoes in their creations today.

11.5. Culinary Heritage: A Timeless Treat

Cypriot cuisine is a gastronomical journey into the island's historical timeline. The culinary practice of serving 'Meze', a selection of small dishes, traces its roots back to the Persian rule. The preoccupation with halloumi cheese is a tradition passed on from the Byzantine era. Commandaria, a sweet dessert wine reputedly the oldest named wine in the world, is still produced in the island's wineries, living testament to a tradition dating back to 800 BC. Each bite and sip in Cyprus narrates a historical tale.

In conclusion, there's a certain serenity and wisdom that permeates Cyprus, an island where time merges the old with the new. As we dwell into its contemporary life, we traverse its ancient past, a journey replete with insights and surprises, making us appreciate the richness of human civilization more than ever before. The echoes of ancient Cyprus continue to reverberate, shaping the island's identity in a world that is constantly changing, reflecting that sometimes to understand the present, and anticipate the future, one needs to hearken to the wisdom of the past.

Printed in Great Britain
by Amazon